VIRTUAL REALITY

and Other Useful Tech

COOL TECH

World Book, Inc.
180 North LaSalle Street
Suite 900
Chicago, Illinois 60601
USA

For information about other "Cool Tech" titles, as well as other World Book print and digital publications, please go to www.worldbook.com.

For information about other World Book publications, call 1-800-WORLDBK (967-5325).

For information about sales to schools and libraries, call 1-800-975-3250 (United States) or 1-800-837-5365 (Canada).

Library of Congress Cataloging-in-Publication Data for this volume has been applied for.

Cool Tech
ISBN: 978-0-7166-2429-5 (set, hc.)

Virtual Reality and Other Useful Tech
ISBN: 978-0-7166-2433-2 (hc.)

Also available as:
ISBN: 978-0-7166-2450-9 (e-book)

2nd printing November 2021

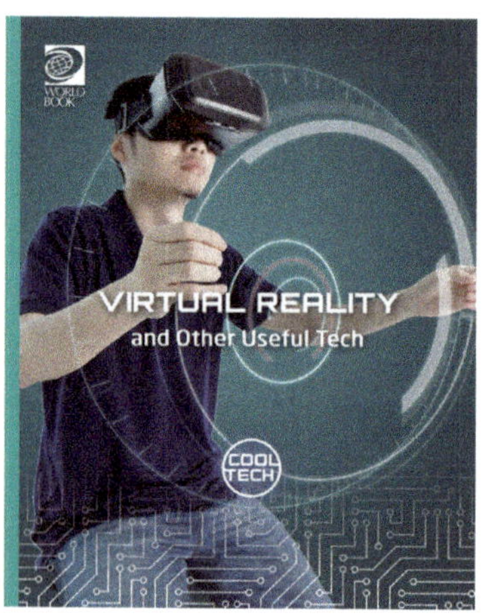

Credit: © Wonry/Getty Images

STAFF

Editorial

Writer
Madeline King

Manager, New Content
Jeff De La Rosa

Manager, New Product Development
Nick Kilzer

Proofreader
Nathalie Strassheim

Manager, Contracts and Compliance (Rights and Permissions)
Loranne K. Shields

Manager, Indexing Services
David Pofelski

Digital

Director, Digital Product Development
Erika Meller

Digital Product Manager
Jonathan Wills

Graphics and Design

Senior Designer
Don DiSante

Media Editor
Rosalia Bledsoe

Manufacturing/Production

Manufacturing Manager
Anne Fritzinger

Production Specialist
Curley Hunter

CONTENTS

Introduction. 5

1 Virtual Reality 6

2 Virtual Assistants 14

3 Personal Transport 18

4 Health Trackers. 26

5 Smart Kitchens. 34

6 Technical Toys 38

7 Holograms and 3D Projections. 42

Glossary 46

Index. 47

Acknowledgments. 48

INTRODUCTION

What do you think of when you hear the words "cool technology"? Do you think of a fusion-powered reactor that can generate virtually unlimited energy? Do you imagine a high-tech spacecraft that will carry future astronauts to the farthest reaches of the solar system? Maybe you picture high-speed trains that will allow commuters to zip between distant cities. All of these technologies sound pretty impressive. But how likely are they to change your life?

Now think about technologies that are somewhat smaller, cheaper, and more readily available. A self-balancing scooter or an ordinary smartwatch may not seem as impressive as fusion or a spaceship. But these useful technologies are much more likely to change your life, at least in the short term.

Inventors are constantly developing useful devices that promise to make our lives easier, more fulfilling, and perhaps a bit more fun. So when you hear "cool tech," don't immediately look to the stars. The coolest tech may be hiding around the corner, in your kitchen, or even on your wrist.

1 VIRTUAL REALITY

EXPLORING IMAGINARY WORLDS

Every now and then, each of us just wants to get away from it all. An escape from reality may involve an exotic vacation, a secluded hideaway, or even just the pages of a good book. But what if we could escape reality entirely—entering an alternate world that exists only inside a computer?

The dream of real escape into an imaginary world has led to the development of **virtual reality,** often abbreviated VR. Virtual reality is an artificial, three-dimensional environment generated by a computer. A VR experience is typically viewed through a headset. The headset replaces what a person normally sees with computer-generated images and sounds. The result is that the user feels as if he or she has entered another place, be it a faraway planet, a time long past, or a world that never existed.

Virtual reality may sound like fun and games—and it can be. But the virtual worlds that people create give form to their imaginations, helping to communicate ideas. An architect, for example, might use virtual reality to allow clients to explore a building before it is even constructed. Virtual environments are also a great place to train for everything from piloting to surgery, removed from real-world dangers.

Through the use of a handheld controller and a headset, a person can explore and interact with a world that exists only inside a computer, called virtual reality.

VR GEAR

Virtual reality (VR) requires a variety of tools, depending on the level of *immersion.* Immersion is a measure of how convincing is the illusion of being in a virtual world. A non-immersive VR experience might involve a number of computer screens and a special controller. A more immersive experience requires a special headset and other accessories.

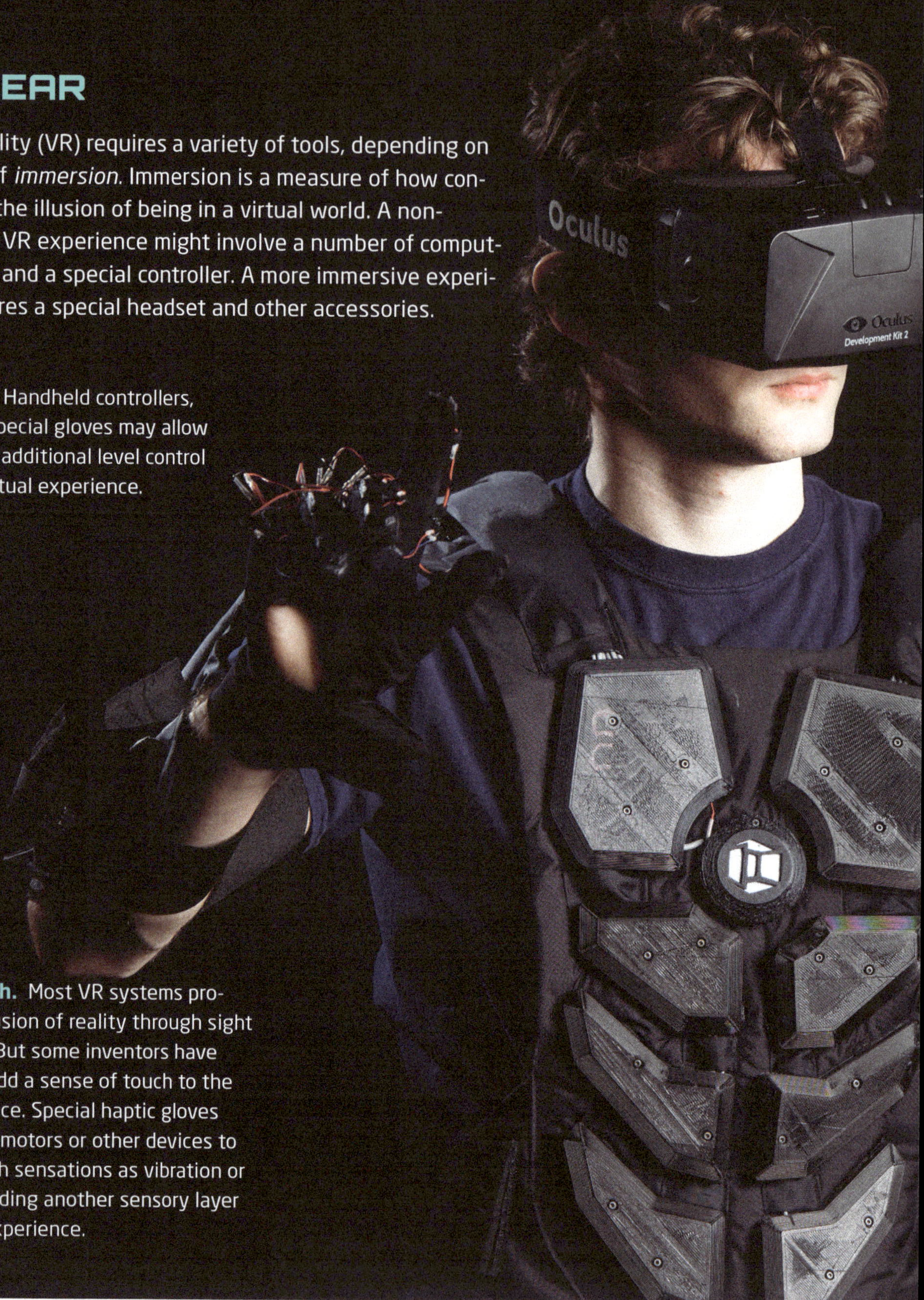

Hands on. Handheld controllers, wands, or special gloves may allow the user an additional level control over the virtual experience.

Get in touch. Most VR systems produce the illusion of reality through sight and sound. But some inventors have worked to add a sense of touch to the VR experience. Special haptic gloves or suits use motors or other devices to produce such sensations as vibration or pressure, adding another sensory layer to the VR experience.

Heads up. An immersive experience requires a special headset known as a **head-mounted display (HMD).** This device includes one or two small display screens and stereo headphones. Motion sensors in the HMD enable the computer to track the user's head movements. When the head is turned in a particular direction, the computer determines what the user sees and hears when looking in that direction. This enables the user to "look around" the virtual world.

19TH-CENTURY VIRTUAL REALITY

During the 1800's and early 1900's, the stereoscope *(above)* was a popular viewing device. It made use of two photographs of a scene taken from slightly different angles. The photographs were mounted side by side and viewed through a combination of lenses and prisms. To the user, the two photographs seem to blend into a single three-dimensional image. Many head-mounted VR displays use a similar trick, presenting the viewer with two small screens or one split-screen image to create the illusion of depth.

Playing in a CAVE. A CAVE system provides a low-immersion VR experience. CAVE stands for *C*ave *A*utomatic *V*irtual *E*nvironment. The system projects images of the virtual world on the floor and walls of a room—the "cave" *(right)*. The images change as the user changes position.

FAKING REALITY

The American computer scientist Jaron Lanier coined the term *virtual reality* (VR) in the late 1980's. Lanier envisioned highly *immersive* (convincing) experiences provided through advanced computer technology. But long before—and since—people have tried to create immersive simulations, with and without the help of computers.

Panoramic paintings. To be fairly immersive, a VR experience must fill a viewer's entire field of vision. For a similar experience, people of the 1800's looked to *panoramas*—360-degree murals that surrounded their viewers with painted imagery. Panoramas aimed to give the viewer a sense of being present at a historical event or scene. Many panoramas are still "around" today.

The Sword of Damocles was the unlikely nickname of what is widely considered the first head-mounted display. It was created in 1968 by the American computer scientist Ivan Sutherland. The device showed simple computer images to each eye, providing a three-dimensional view that changed with the viewer's head position. The massive headset dangled by mechanical arm over the user's head *(right),* much as the mythical sword hung precariously above the head of Damocles.

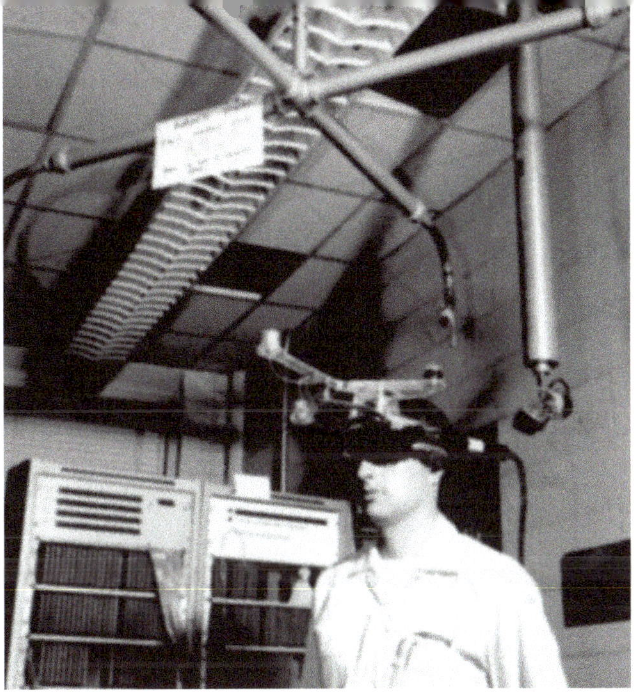

Sensorama. In the mid-1900's, the filmmaker Morton Heilig created the Sensorama *(left).* It was an arcade-style theater cabinet that surrounded the user in the sights, sounds, and smells of a variety of experiences. The experiences included riding a motorcycle and being stuck in a bottle of soda. To fully immerse users in these experiences, the Sensorama included speakers, fans, scent generators, and a vibrating chair.

Cheap VR. Virtual reality equipment is famously expensive. The technology company Google demonstrated a cheaper way when it introduced Google Cardboard *(right)* in 2014. Cardboard is an origami headset made from—you guessed it—cardboard and some cheap lenses. Attaching Cardboard to an ordinary **smartphone** created a do-it-yourself head-mounted display.

USES OF VIRTUAL REALITY

Perhaps the best-known use of virtual reality (VR) is in entertainment, particularly electronic games. But VR technology has more serious uses as well. Here are just a few examples of the many uses for which virtual reality is being developed.

Virtual reality can help a soldier to train for combat *(below)* or an automotive engineer to refine a design before the first part goes into production *(right)*.

Design. Virtual reality can give shape to the imaginations of designers, enabling clients and others to explore their creations long before construction has begun. Architects can show visitors around a building before a single brick has been laid. Automobile designers have used virtual reality to inspect their creations inside and out before manufacturing even one part.

Training. In virtual reality, people can train to do difficult and dangerous things safely removed from real-life consequences. For example, the militaries of the United States and other countries have used VR to help soldiers train for combat. VR technology has also been used to train astronauts for space missions. Surgeons may practice in virtual reality to prepare for a difficult medical procedure.

Medical treatment. Medical professionals have experimented with virtual reality in the treatment of a number of conditions, including post-traumatic stress disorder (PTSD). PTSD is a psychological illness in which a person repeatedly remembers, relives, or dreams about a terrible experience. Virtual reality can help in the healing process by allowing patients to relive a traumatic experience under the close control and supervision of a qualified therapist.

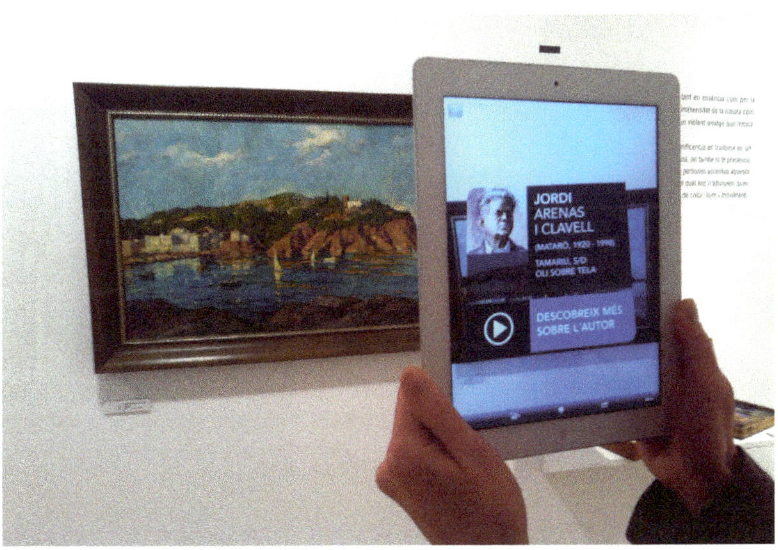

Augmented reality. Elements of VR technology are useful in a related technology called **augmented reality (AR).** Instead of seeing an immersive virtual world, an AR user sees the world around them overlaid with virtual details generated by a computer. Pointing an AR display at a painting, for example, might cause the display to show the painting's title, creator, and other information.

2 VIRTUAL ASSISTANTS

WISHES GRANTED

Virtual reality can take us to some amazing places. But many of us need help right here, in the real world. Remember the story of Aladdin? Aladdin is a poor boy who finds a magical lamp. According to the folk tale, the lamp held a powerful spirit called a *jinni* (sometimes spelled *genie).* The spirit, who was bound to grant the wishes of the lamp's owner, became the key to solving Aladdin's problems.

Magic lamps and jinni are the stuff of folklore. But inventors may have developed the next best thing—the **virtual assistant.** A virtual assistant is a voice-activated computer program, often accessed through a smartphone or a computerized device called a **smart speaker** *(far left).* A virtual assistant can answer questions, play music on request, and make purchases online. It can even control such household devices as lighting and locks over a computer network.

Many people and households already make use of a virtual assistant, such as Apple's Siri, Amazon Alexa, or Microsoft's Cortana. As virtual assistants become more widespread and sophisticated, more and more of our wishes can be granted Aladdin-stye—just by saying the words.

IBM Shoebox. In 1961, the computer company IBM launched the Shoebox, the first **digital** speech recognition tool. While it could only recognize 16 words, the Shoebox sparked decades of innovation in speech recognition technology. Today, smart speakers can recognize millions of words.

A HELPFUL SPIRIT

Think of a virtual assistant as your own version of Aladdin's jinni, ready at the call of your voice to answer a question, schedule an appointment, or order dinner. Users ask questions or give commands to virtual assistants, for example "Alexa, what is the weather like today?" or "Hey Siri, add milk to the grocery list."

Wake up! A virtual assistant is generally activated using a special command or greeting called a "wake word." The virtual assistant will listen without responding until it hears the wake word. Examples include "Alexa," for Amazon's Alexa and "Hey, Siri," for Apple's Siri. Once the device hears this wake word, it begins recording your speech and uses the internet to interpret and fulfill your requests.

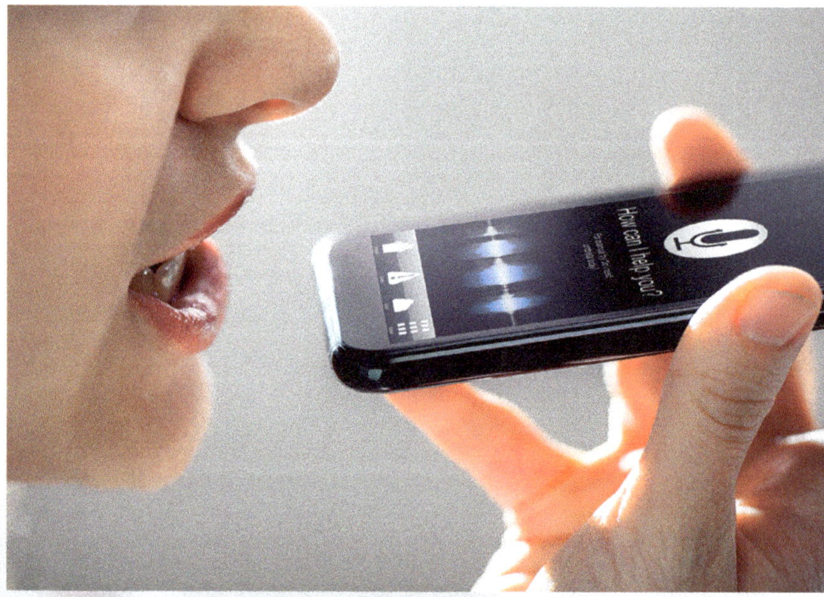

Magic word. Many parents have become worried that barking commands at virtual assistants can train kids to be rude in their interactions with people. Amazon had a solution. It is called the "magic word" feature. When a kid adds "please" to their request, the virtual assistant thanks them for asking so nicely.

The magic lamp. Virtual assistants can be accessed using a smartphone. But the technology really began to take off with the introduction of the smart speaker *(below)*. The smart speaker is a compact household device that includes a speaker and microphone. It can be used to play music or other sounds, but its primary purpose is to provide access to a virtual assistant.

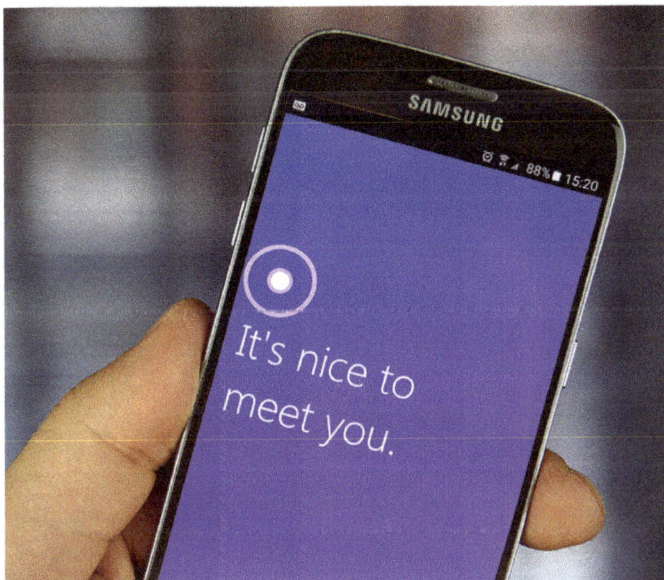

Always listening. Virtual assistants are passive listening devices. That means that their microphones are always on. For some people, this feature raises privacy concerns. They fear that the virtual assistant is recording everything they say. The recordings could be stolen by hackers or used unethically by technology companies.

3 PERSONAL TRANSPORTS

GETTING AROUND IN STYLE

Virtual assistants can help to summon goods and services to your location. But what happens when there is somewhere else you have to be? For long-distance travel, there are planes, trains, and automobiles. But when it comes to plain old getting around, for much of human history we have been largely limited to putting one foot in front of the other.

Technology has begun to change all that. Say you need to get around the block or even just from one side to the other of a large warehouse or factory. Today, you have more options than ever before. There are scooters of various shapes and sizes and even self-balancing vehicles that will not tip over.

Some day, we may even leave wheels—and the ground—behind. Inventors have dreamed for years of developing **hoverboards—**skateboardlike craft that float through the air.

SCOOTERS

People around the world use scooters for a variety of reasons. They are low cost and are a small size. Scooters are especially popular in cities, because they can navigate narrow streets and congested traffic. Scooters are also fuel efficient. For this reason, some people use scooters as their primary means of transportation.

The first scooter. In 1894, Hildebrand and Wolfmüller designed the first scooterlike vehicle. A few years later, manufacturers in France, the United Kingdom, and the United States were making scooters. The vehicles came increasingly popular after World War II (1939-1945). While traditional scooters are still used today, rechargeable electric scooters have become very popular.

The Vespa. One of the most famous scooter manufacturers is Piaggio. The company is known for creating the Vespa. It was a response to the need for an affordable, inexpensive form of transportation for many people. In the 1940's, it was a revolutionary vehicle for women, because they could ride it in skirts. The Vespa continues to be popular today *(above).*

Razor scooter. One of the most famous scooters is the Razor scooter *(below)*. Created in 2000, the Razor is popular among kids and adults alike. It is lightweight and foldable, making it easy to ride and to store. It is useful for travel and, of course, play. But don't go looking for a gas tank or charging cord—the razor is powered by the push of the human foot.

Electric scooters dot the landscape, in many big cities, thanks to such companies as Bird and Lime. They have introduced scooter-sharing programs in cities all over the world. Such programs allow users to pick up a scooter wherever they need it and drop it off at their destination. Like the Razor Scooter, electric scooters *(above)* are light and compact, able to make their way through congested traffic.

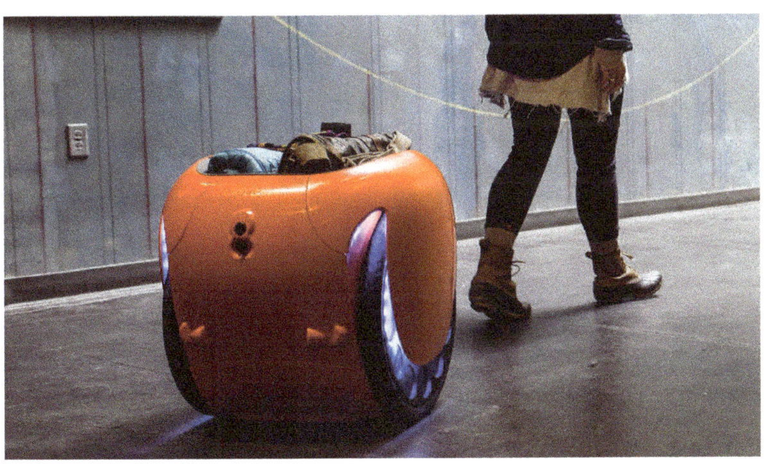

Scooters aren't just for people! Sometimes our stuff needs to get places, too. That's why Piaggio has created a rolling robot to carry items. The robot, called Gita *(left)*, holds up to 40 pounds of cargo and follows its user to assist in such tasks as picking up groceries.

HOVERBOARDS

When it comes to moving in style, what could be cooler than a skateboard? How about a skateboard without wheels, gliding smoothly along on a cushion of thin air? This kind of vehicle is called a hoverboard. Practical models have yet to be invented, but people have dreamed of hoverboards for years.

Flying platform. In the 1950's, Hiller Aircraft created the first object truly resembling a hoverboard. While it was a very rudimentary version of today's hoverboards, it sparked years of attempts at making hoverboards. To use the Flying Platform, the user leaned in one direction and the platform would follow. Like the Segway self-balancing scooter that came decades later, the Flying Platform could not fall, because the platform would move upright and slow down.

Small, rechargeable self-balancing scooters *(far right)* are often called hoverboards, but they do not truly float above the ground.

Hendo Hoverboard. One attempt at a real-life hoverboard is the Hendo Hoverboard. Created by Greg and Jill Henderson, the Hendo Hoverboard is more like the hoverboard seen in the "Back to the Future" motion pictures (1985-1990). Unlike some wheeled devices that call themselves hoverboards, the Hendo Hoverboard floats above a conductive surface using magnetic technology.

Inspired by pop culture. In *Back to the Future Part II* (released in 1989), the lead character Marty McFly zooms through the city of Hill Valley on a hoverboard in the then-future year of 2015. The year came and went without the imagined hoverboards. But many inventors have been inspired by the movie to create their own models.

SEGWAY

While the destinations may change—Willis Tower in Chicago, the Uffizi Gallery in Florence, or Olympic Park in Beijing—many tourists see these attractions via the same vehicle: the Segway. Now a form of transportation used almost exclusively by tourists and police officers, the Segway was supposed to change the world. When it was unveiled in 2001, technology insiders thought it was going to be even more revolutionary than the personal computer.

Dean Kamen created the Segway to be the "human transporter." He wanted it to be the bridge between walking and driving a car. The user stands upright on a platform and maneuvers the device with the handlebars. Users are not supposed to—or even physically able to—fall off the device. Although the machine's design *looks* quite simple, it contains a complicated system of **gyroscopes** and balance technology. The Segway appealed to environmental concerns, because it delivered zero emissions.

While the Segway's namesake—*segue*—means to move smoothly from one situation to another, the Segway's transition to the consumer market was anything but smooth. Two years after its debut, people questioned its use. It was too bulky and fast for sidewalks, but too small and slow for roadways. In 2002, many states in the United States passed legislation to allow Segways on sidewalks. Another problem arose in 2003 when the company recalled 6,000 Segways, because riders fell off when the batteries were low.

The Segway did not rival the success or popularity of the personal computer. While they can be seen carrying wide-eyed tourists from monument to monument, they are not as widely used as the creators had hoped.

WONDROUS WHEELCHAIR

The Segway was not Kamen's first invention. In the late 1990's, Kamen introduced the iBOT. It is a six-wheeled motorized wheelchair that allows users to do a task that had been almost impossible: climb stairs. The device also lifts users to eye level.

4 HEALTH TRACKERS

TIME FOR A CHECKUP—ON YOURSELF!

Most people would like to develop healthful habits. Some of us would like to eat a more nutritious diet. Others want to get more exercise each day or more sleep each night. For people with certain medical conditions, controlling such health indicators as blood pressure or blood sugar may be the key to staying out of the hospital.

Our good intentions may start us on a journey to lifelong health. But how will we know whether we are making progress toward our goals? And who will alert us when we start to slip? Technology has begun to provide an answer—in the form of health trackers.

Health trackers are devices or computer programs that monitor various indicators of health. A health tracker may measure your heart rate, count the number of steps you take, or even keep track of how many times you wake during the night. With new trackers being developed every day, we will soon know more about our health than people just a few years ago could possIbly ImagIne.

Wearable technology. Many health trackers can be worn on the body. But health trackers are far from the first wearable technology. Some of the most interesting wearable technologies of the past include the air-conditioned top hat and the abacus ring. A newer technology that is truly wearable is so-called smart clothing. The Nadi X Yoga Pants, for example, have sensors on the hips, knees, and ankles. The sensors alert you when you need to correct your yoga pose.

WEARABLE FITNESS TRACKERS

Fitness trackers for your wrist are popular. They are lightweight and convenient. And, thanks to various colors, textures, and designs, they can even be quite fashionable. Popular brands include Fitbit, Garmin, and TomTom. They differ in appearance and, in some cases, features. Here are some of the indicators such a tracker may measure or monitor.

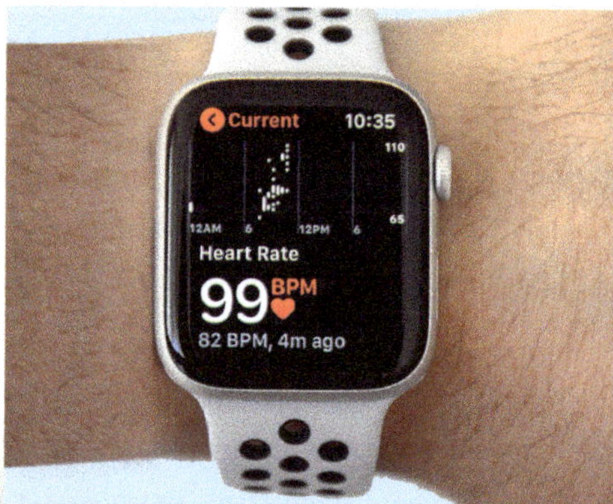

Temperature. When your body heat rises, your fitness tracker may know that you are exerting yourself. If heart rate does not also rise, however, the tracker may warn that you could be getting sick.

Heart rate. Optical heart-rate monitors measure heart rate using light. The light is a light-emitting diode, or LED. The LED shines through your skin, and an optical sensor analyzes the light that bounces back. Blood absorbs light, so changes in light level correspond to heart rate.

Sweat. Galvanic response sensors measure the electrical conductivity of your skin. When you sweat, your skin better conducts electricity, and the sensors will detect that. Sweating gives the sensors information about what you are doing, so the fitness tracker can do its job.

Motion. Health professionals recommend walking about 10,000 steps each day. A device called an accelerometer records the steps to reach this goal. It measures orientation and acceleration to determine when and how you are moving. The data is converted into step counts and other activity reports.

Ambient light. Your smartphone dims the screen at night and brightens it in the sun. Fitness trackers also have this feature—using devices called ambient light sensors.

Ultraviolet (UV) light. Overexposure to UV rays can lead to sunburn and even skin cancer. Some fitness trackers have UV sensors to alert the user when they are absorbing harmful UV radiation. The fitness tracker warns when you are likely to burn.

Location. The Global Positioning System (GPS) uses satellites to pinpoint someone's exact location. With GPS in a wearable fitness tracker, users can map their exercise routes and analyze the terrain of the area in which they are working out.

WATCHING YOUR WEIGHT

It can be tough to control your weight or to shed excess pounds. When the battle of the bulge gets tough, people often turn to technology to help them win the war on weight.

Wacky weight-loss devices. Mechanisms for losing weight are not a new phenomenon. Advertisements from as far back as the 1920's show technology that was revolutionary at the time. Dr. Walter's Famous Medicated Reducing Rubber Garments promised weight loss, thanks to the rubber band around your waist that would cause you to supposedly sweat away the calories. Dr. Lawton's Fat Reducer was another device. It was designed like a plunger and worked like a vacuum—sucking out extra fat. Hardly any of these devices worked. Many were dangerous, as well.

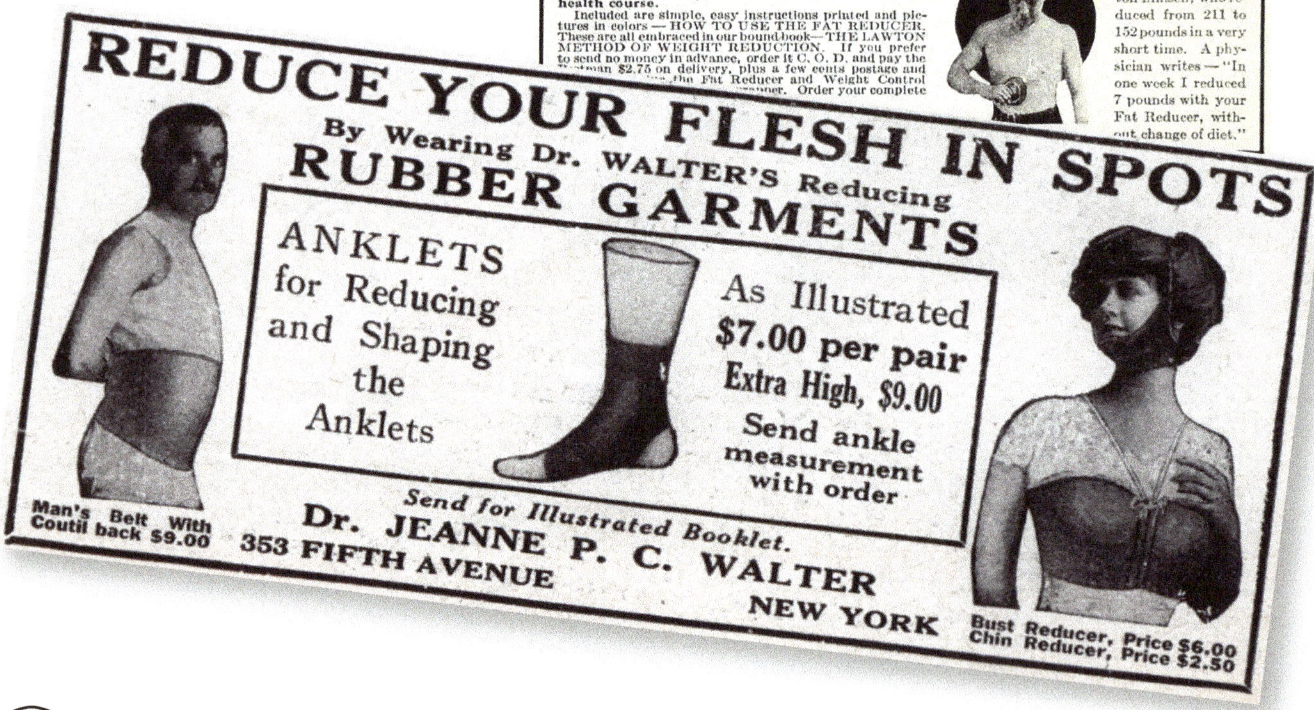

SmartPlate is a more modern weight-loss device. It looks like many other plates. But it is unlike your everyday ceramic or paper plate, because it has technology: scales and digital cameras. When you put food on the plate, the scales and cameras weigh and take pictures of your meal. Then the high-tech plate gets nutritional information from a U.S. Department of Agriculture database. The information on calorie count is sent to your smartphone. Bon appétit!

WearSens. The inventors of WearSens think this calorie-counting necklace is the perfect accessory to complete any outfit! The necklace uses piezoelectricity technology. That means it uses technology that uses crystals to change mechanical energy into electricity. The technology tracks vibrations from food you eat. Different foods cause different vibrations. Sensors record these movements. The results are then sent to your smartphone.

Newspaper advertisements from the early 1900's *(opposite)* crow about the "high-tech" weight loss fads of years past.

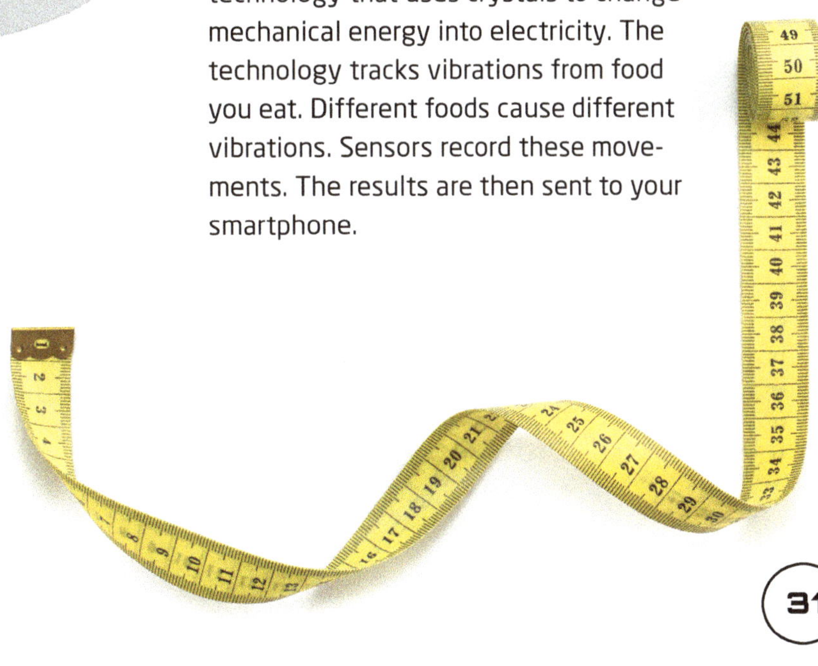

A BRIEF HISTORY OF SLEEP

What could be easier than getting a little shut-eye? Yet millions of people do not get enough sleep each night. The result is worse than just a few yawns and a pair of blood-shot eyes. Tired people are less productive and far more likely to get into accidents. Perhaps that is why people have long turned to technology to help provide restful sleep.

The humble bed is one of the oldest pieces of technology in use. The use of beds dates back to the Neolithic period—that's 10,000 years ago! In ancient Egypt, pharaohs whad elaborate beds, while common people slept on a heap of palms. The ancient Romans developed the first luxury bed. Gold, silver, and bronze adorned the frame and mattresses were stuffed with reeds, hay, wool, or feathers.

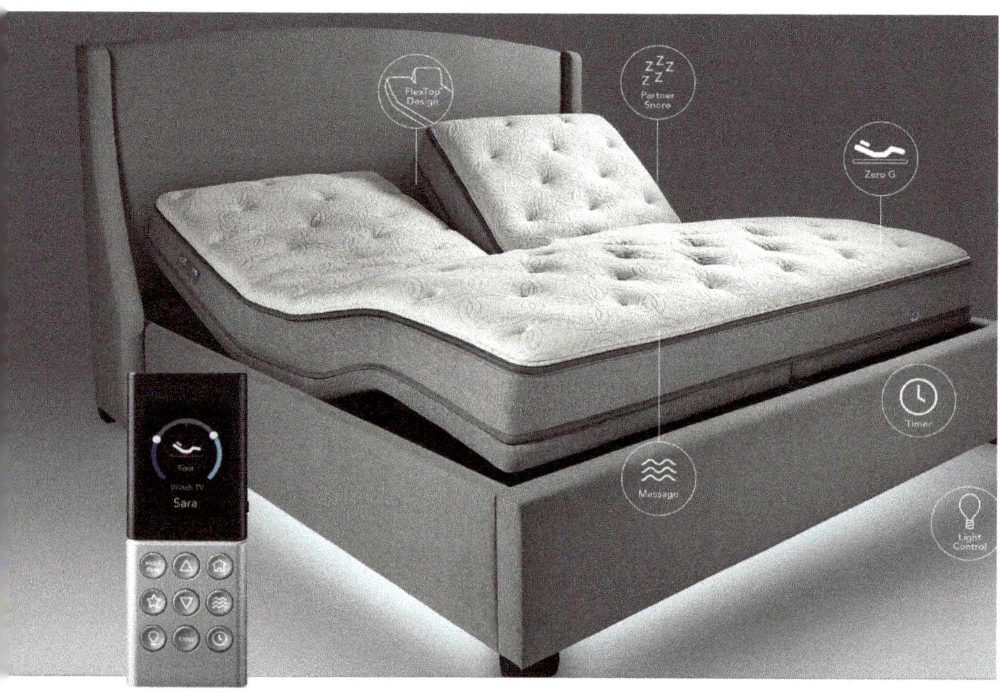

A smart mattress optimizes the way you sleep by tracking your sleep patterns. Sleep Number created a bed that has sensors to track your heart rate, breathing, and sleep restfulness. After compiling the data, it gives personalized suggestions to improve your sleep.

Don't forget baby! Getting a good night's sleep is not just about being comfortable. Parents can lose sleep worrying about the well-being of their children. Baby monitors were developed to help insure that both babies and their parents can get restful, worry-free Z's.

Radio Nurse. In 1937, the first baby monitor was available to the masses. It was called the Radio Nurse. It was very similar to modern-day baby monitors. One important piece of the device was the "Guardian Ear." It was plugged in somewhere in the baby's room, while the Radio Nurse was in a place where the parents could hear.

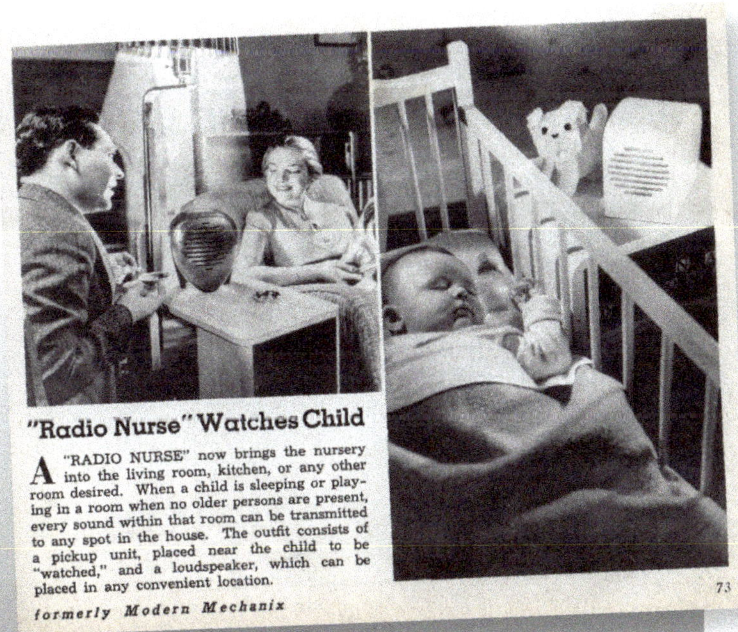

"Radio Nurse" Watches Child

A "RADIO NURSE" now brings the nursery into the living room, kitchen, or any other room desired. When a child is sleeping or playing in a room when no older persons are present, every sound within that room can be transmitted to any spot in the house. The outfit consists of a pickup unit, placed near the child to be "watched," and a loudspeaker, which can be placed in any convenient location.

73

formerly Modern Mechanix

Owlet is a baby monitor that uses advanced technology. It looks like a sock, fitting easily onto a baby's foot. The device tracks heart rate and oxygen levels. It then sends the information to the parents' smartphones.

5 SMART KITCHENS

The kitchen of the future features a variety of smart devices that monitor the condition of stored foods, offer cooking suggestions, assist in preparation, and more.

WHAT'S COOKING?

When some people think of a kitchen, they may reminisce about family recipes passed down through generations or sitting and talking while a delicious meal cooks slowly on the stovetop. But other people see the kitchen as a place of hard, hot work and even toil. Inventors are looking to change this, taking the decision-making, time, and in some cases even the cooking out of cooking.

Foodini. Using **3D-printing** technology, a device called the Foodini enables the user to print food in specific portions and shapes. The creators think the Foodini can help users to cook creative and tastier meals. Another selling point of the device is health. One feature may cause the machine to stop printing food once it reaches a certain calorie count. This is intended to provide portion control and help users reach their health goals.

GET SMART!

What does it mean for technology to be smart? **Smart devices** use computers and computer networks to help us manage our lives. Consider an ordinary refrigerator. It's pretty much just a cold box you keep your food in. But a smart refrigerator might tell you when foods are about to expire, help you make a shopping list, and even link with a wearable fitness tracker to recommend meals or snacks. Smart cabinets might monitor the foods you keep in them, and smart ovens could give you ideas for cooking them. Experts believe that the smart kitchen is years away, but such companies as Whirlpool have already started on plans.

June Oven. One popular smart oven is the June Oven. While it bakes, broils, and roasts like ordinary ovens, it is very different. Users can watch their meal cook, thanks to built-in cameras. The oven also has an app which sends notifications to your smartphone.

Smart ovens. Complete with **Wi-Fi** or Bluetooth, a smart oven is an electric range that connects to your smartphone. Smart ovens may cook food more evenly than a conventional oven. Users can adjust the cooking temperature and time without ever touching the oven.

Smart refrigerators connect to the internet and, in some cases, other smart devices like smart speakers and smart TV's. Their touchscreens act as the stage on which users can utilize the smart refrigerator features. Some of these features are coordinating schedules with members of the family, looking up recipes, and setting notifi-cations to inform you when food has expired.

THE MICROWAVE

The machine you use to make delicious, buttery popcorn was discovered by accident. And has its roots in World War II (1939-1945). During the war, scientists invented the magnetron, a device that produced microwaves. Magnetrons were put to work in *radar* (radio detection and ranging) systems. A few years later, a radar engineer named Percy LeBaron Spencer noticed that a candy bar in his pocket had melted after working next to a magnetron. Microwaves had melted the candy! By 1967, microwave ovens for homes were on the market.

6 TECHNOLOGICAL TOYS

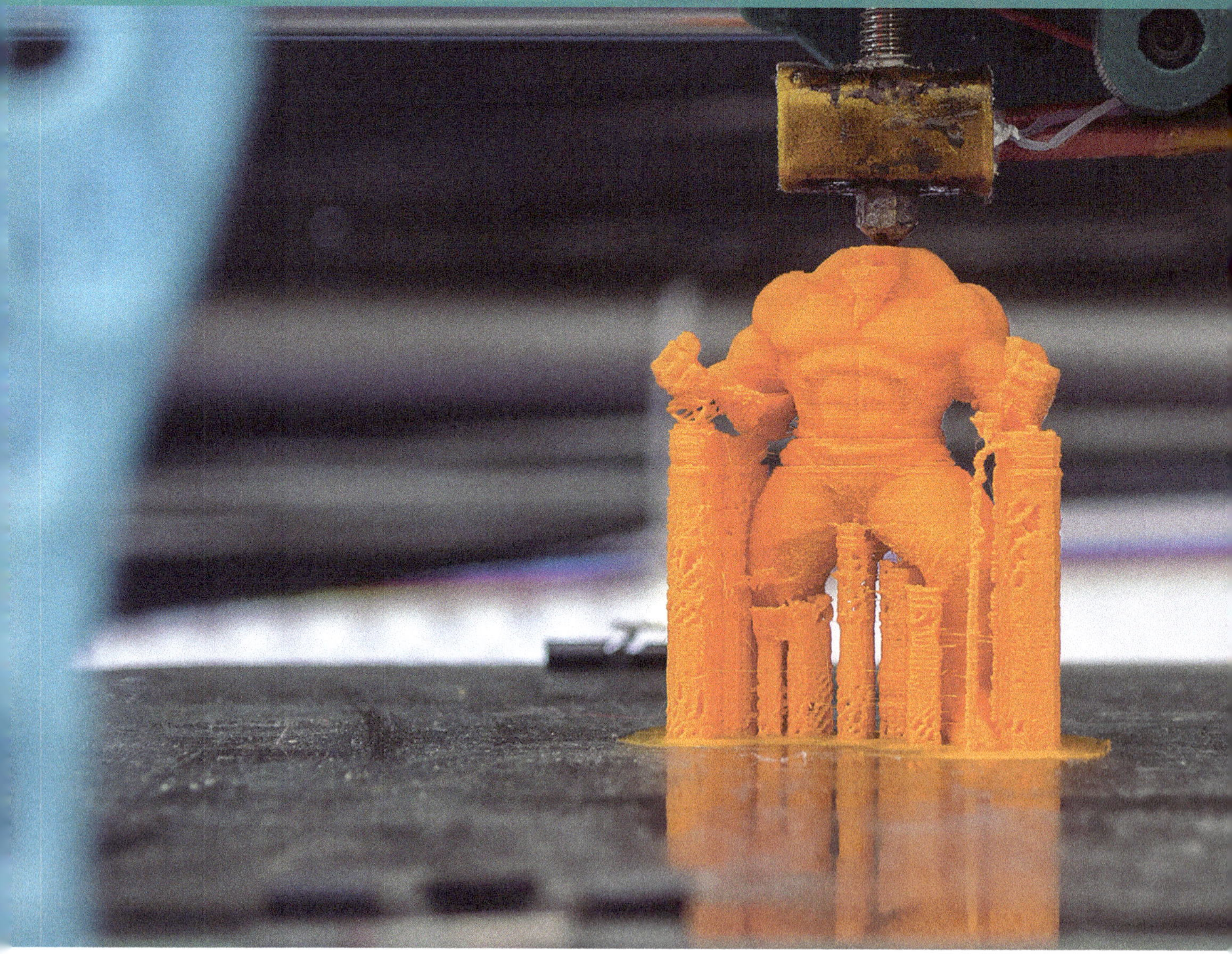

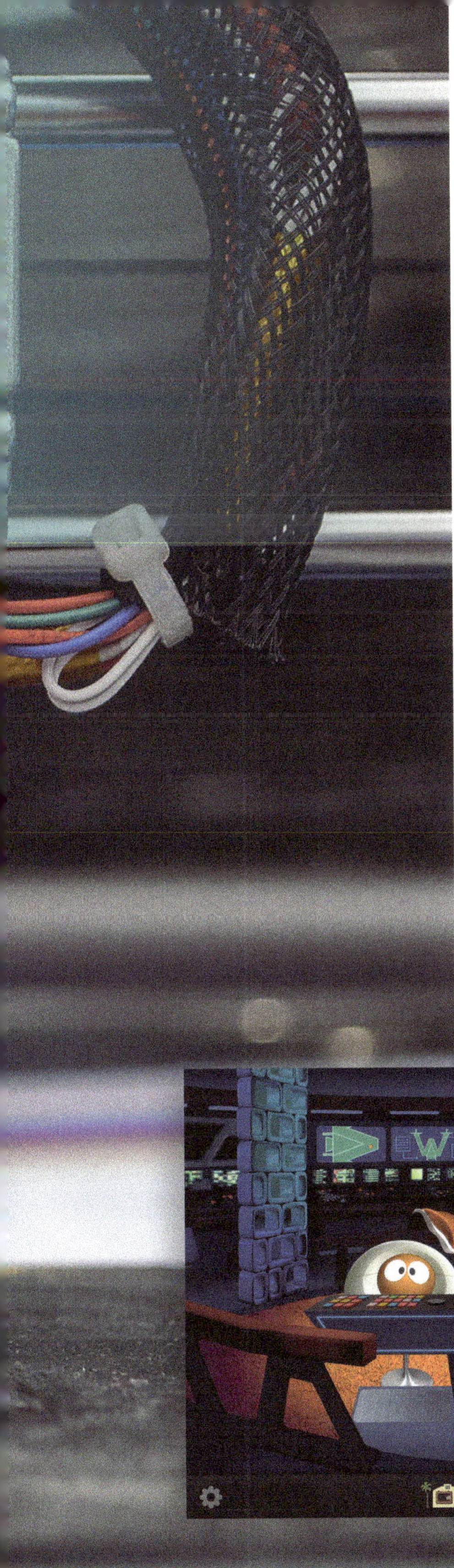

PLAYTIME 2.0

Smart kitchen technology is about as useful as it gets. But what good is useful tech if you can't have a little fun? Today's toymakers have more technology at their fingertips than ever before. And they're using it to create some of the most amazing toys ever. You can even get in on the action! Devices called 3D printers *(left)* enable users to design and print their own playthings.

Robot playmates are no longer just the stuff of science fiction, with toymakers developing a range of sophisticated models. One example is Cozmo, a tiny toy robot that uses his forklift like arm to play games, by pushing, stacking, and flipping special blocks. With his animated eyes and lively chirps, Cozmo is designed to mimic human feelings, including happiness and frustration. Lose a game to Cozmo, and the robot might celebrate with a victory dance.

ToyTalk. Children throughout the ages have talked to their toys. But the toys haven't always been able to talk back. One company exploring tech toys that talk is the company ToyTalk. ToyTalk has developed apps that allow young people to have a conversation with virtual characters. And now the tech is being adopted by such popular toy lines as Barbie and Thomas the Tank Engine and Friends.

TECH TOYS THROUGH TIME

Technological toys are nothing new. In ancient Africa, kids enjoyed playing with balls, toy animals, and pull toys. Kids in ancient Greece and Rome had fun with boats, carts, hoops, and tops. In the Middle Ages in Europe, popular toys included clay marbles, rattles, and puppets. Though they may seem simple now, each of these toys took advantage of the technology of the day. And as technology has improved, the toys have gotten more fun. Here are just a few highlights.

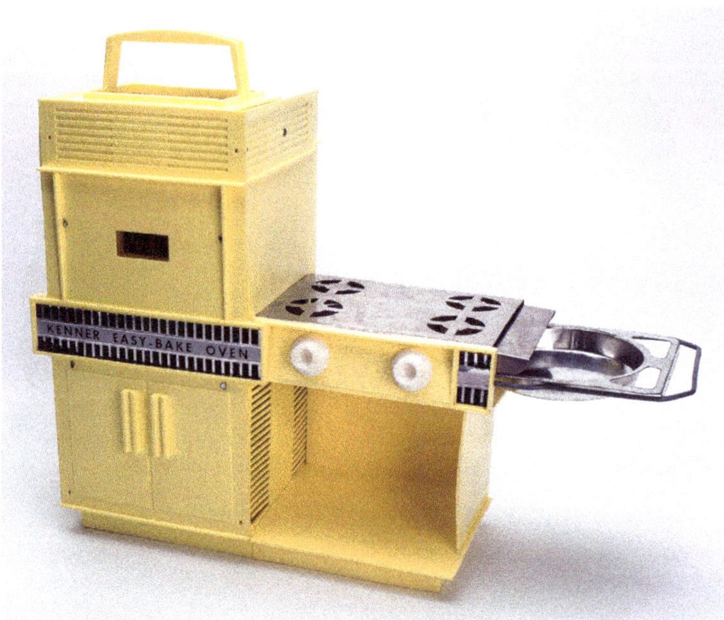

The Easy-Bake Oven *(above)* made its debut in 1963. And while the toy could not prepare an entire dinner, it could prepare children for a lifetime of kitchen chores. Complete with cake mixes and pans, the oven came with recipes for such favorite desserts as chocolate chip cookies, red velvet cake, and sugar cookies. Early Easy-Bake Oven models warmed their treats using the waste heat from a traditional incandescent light bulb. More recent versions include a true electrical heating element.

Magnavox Odyssey was the great-grandfather of modern video game devices. Invented in 1972, the Odyssey *(below)* was a home video game system. It also came with more traditional forms of entertainment: dice, decks of cards, and poker chips. Although the Magnavox Odyssey was not a commercial success, it inspired future home video game systems.

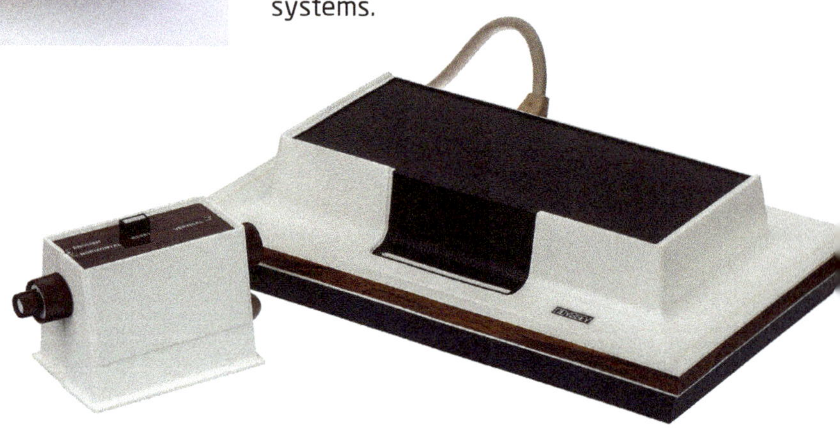

Your Cue to have fun. Some of the best tech toys enable children to learn as they play. The educational robot Cue *(above)*, released in 2017, could talk and play games. But Cue was also designed to teach coding. Cue came with a computer app that featured a special "adventure mode," guiding the user through a series of coding challenges.

Move over, Rover. In the early 2000's, the family dog got a little competition from a new pet, the robot AIBO. AIBO was designed to learn and respond to its owner just like a real pup. From 1999 to 2006, the Sony Corporation of Tokyo, Japan, marketed various AIBO models that could answer to their names and navigate their surroundings. They could also learn to obey dozens of commands, including such canine classics as speak, sit, and stay.

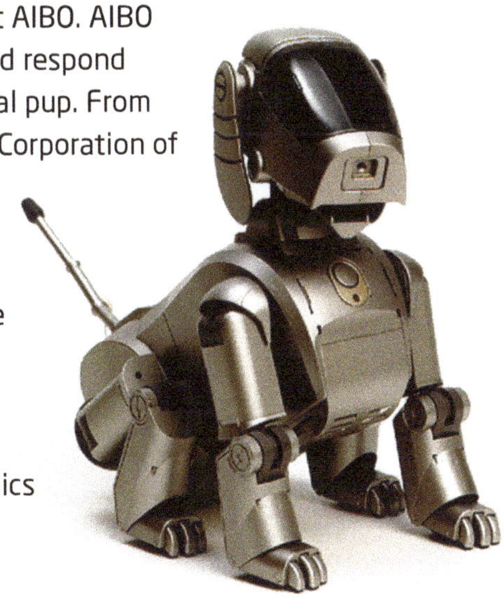

7 HOLOGRAMS AND 3D PROJECTIONS

MAKING THE VIRTUAL REAL

VR and AR are great, but the viewing screen and glasses will always get in your way. What if you could be immersed in a three-dimensional virtual experience without goggles strapped to your face or peering through a screen?

Holography is the most well-known method of projecting a three-dimensional image. A holographic image, called a hologram, is created by scanning an object with a **laser** beam. The reflected light, along with light split from the beam before it reached the object, are recorded on a special film or sensor. Under certain lighting, the image will display, appearing to float either directly behind or in front of the viewing screen. Dennis Gabor, a Hungarian-born engineer, developed holography in 1947. He won the 1971 Nobel Prize in physics for his invention.

Working-class hologram. Believe it or not, holograms are all around us. But they're not used for immersive wonderlands or heart-pounding action experiences. There are holograms on driver's licenses, identification cards, and credit cards. Held up to the light, these shiny, rainbow-colored images present the illusion of depth. Though such holograms are quite mundane, they prevent counterfeiting, as the three-dimensional images are difficult to recreate.

HOLOGRAMS TODAY AND TOMORROW

Future holographic displays must overcome two main obstacles. First, a hologram can't really pop up off its screen. Say you're looking at a hologram from off to the side of the display. The image would be cut off at the edge of the display, ruining the illusion of depth. Second, not much holographic content has been created yet. You can't just tune into The Hologram Channel. Different devices have different ideas on how to sidestep these limitations.

Pepper's ghost still haunting hologram developers. In 2012, rapper Tupac Shakur appeared onstage at the Coachella music festival. This wouldn't have been unusual in itself, but Tupac had died in 1996. Was this a next-generation holographic projection? Actually, the technique used to create the illusion was not holography, but Pepper's ghost, named for the British scientist John Henry Pepper who popularized the trick in the mid-1800's. To dazzle 2012 audiences, a recording of Tupac was projected offstage onto a sheet of glass. This image, in turn, was projected onto a see-through screen placed diagonally across the stage. While Pepper's ghost is an ingenious illusion, the elaborate physical setup needed makes it impractical for home use. But many viewers thought Tupac's late appearance at Coachella was a "hologram."

Through the Looking Glass. The Looking Glass is a box like display that allows people to view a holograph. With special controllers and sensors, users can manipulate or interact with the hologram. The screens are relatively small, but the Looking Glass's designers see it mostly as a tool for 3D creators to see how their creations will look, not necessarily as a consumer product. But these creators will be making some of the first holographic films and games, possibly as content for future commercial-focused Looking Glass displays.

Huge fields of light. Another company plans to avoid screen cutoff problems simply by making enormous holographic screens. Light Field Lab is creating prototype displays just a few inches or centimeters per side. It plans to scale up the technology to create much larger panels. Light Field Lab envisions selling these huge holographic panels to museums and entertainment venues. Such places could sponsor the creation of their own special holographic content.

THE HOLODECK

Long-haul travel in outer space would get boring after a while. In the sci-fi universe of "Star Trek," crew members can train and relax special rooms called holodecks. Vast stories and lush environments can be recreated with holography. Users can interact through voice commands and even through touch. The holodeck's technology is still far beyond what is within reach today, but it continues to inspire inventors and engineers.

GLOSSARY

augmented reality (AR) the addition of artificial visual, auditory, or other sensory information to the physical world, so that it appears to be part of the actual environment.

digital all types of electronic equipment and applications that use information in the form of numeric code.

gyroscope a device that uses rotation to produce a stable direction in space.

head-mounted display (HMD) a device that contains one or two small display screens and stereo headphones. The HMD can be a helmet, goggles, lightweight glasses, or a framework that holds a smartphone or other portable device in front of a user's face.

hoverboard a futuristic skateboard without wheels, that glides smoothly on a cushion of air.

laser a device that produces a very narrow and intense beam of a very narrow range of light wavelengths going in only one direction. By contrast, a standard light source produces light of many wavelengths all traveling in slightly different directions.

smart device any device with at least one embedded computer chip that can perform various functions and respond to simple commands.

smart speaker a small computer that has a microphone and speaker but usually no screen. A smart speaker is loaded with voice assistant software that allows its user to find information on the internet and control connected devices with voice commands.

smartphone a portable telephone equipped to perform additional functions beyond calling, such as providing internet access, supporting text messaging, or taking photographs.

3D printing a manufacturing technology that creates three-dimensional (3D) objects from computer instructions.

virtual assistant a voice-activated computer program that can perform various functions such as, answering questions, playing music, and making purchases online.

virtual reality an artificial, three-dimensional computer environment.

Wi-Fi wireless internet access. The ability to connect to internet services without the use of cables.

INDEX

A
AIBO (robot), 41
Amazon (company), 15-17
Apple Inc., 15, 16
augmented reality (AR), 13, 43

B
baby monitors, 33
"Back To the Future" movies, 23
beds, 32

C
CAVE systems, 9
clothing, smart, 27
combat training, 12
computers, 7-10, 15, 24, 36
Cozmo (robot), 39
Cue (robot), 41

E
Easy-Bake Oven, 40

F
fitness trackers, 28-29
Flying Platform, 22
Foodini, 35

G
Gabor, Dennis, 43
Gita (robot), 21
Global Positioning System (GPS), 29
Google Cardboard, 11

H
head-mounted displays (HMD's), 9, 11
headsets, 7, 9, 11
health trackers, 25-31
Heilig, Morton, 11
Hendo Hoverboard, 23
holodecks, 45
holograms, 43-45
hoverboards, 19, 22-23

I
IBM Shoebox, 15
iBOT wheelchair, 25
immersion, 8, 9

J
June Oven, 36

K
Kamen, Dean, 24, 25
kitchens, smart, 34-37

L
Lanier, Jaron, 10
Light Field Lab (company), 45
Looking Glass, 44

M
magic word feature, 17
Magnavox Odyssey, 40
magnetrons, 37
medicine, 12, 13
microwave ovens, 37

N
Nadi X Yoga Pants, 27

O
ovens, smart, 36
Owlet baby monitor, 33

P
panoramas, 10
Pepper, John Henry, 44
Pepper's ghost, 44
personal transports, 18-25
Piaggio (company), 20, 21
post-traumatic stress disorder (PTSD), 13
privacy, 17

R
Radio Nurse, 33
Razor scooter, 21
refrigerators, smart, 36, 37
robots, 21, 39, 41

S
scooters, 20-21
Segway, 22, 24-25
Sensorama, 11
Shakur, Tupac, 44
sleep devices, 32-33
Sleep Number (company), 32
smart devices, 36
smart speakers, 14-15, 17, 37
smartphones, 11, 15-17, 29, 36
SmartPlate, 31
Sony Corporation, 41
Spencer, Percy LeBaron, 37
"Star Trek" (series), 45
stereoscopes, 9
Sutherland, Ivan, 11
Sword of Damocles (headset), 11

T
3D images. *See* holograms; virtual reality (VR)
3D printing, 35, 38-39
toys, 38-41
ToyTalk, 39

U
ultraviolet (UV) radiation, 29

V
Vespa (scooter), 29
video games, 40
virtual assistants, 14-17
virtual reality (VR), 6-13, 43

W
wake words, 16
WearSens, 31
weight-loss devices, 30-31

ACKNOWLEDGMENTS

5 © Syda Productions/Shutterstock

6-7 © David McNew, Getty Images

8-9 © J. Adam Fenster, University of Rochester; © Pattarapong Kumlert, Shutterstock; © Visbox, Inc.

10-11 © Tim Brown, Alamy Images; © Morton Heilig; © Harvard University; © Misszin/Shutterstock

12-13 John F. Williams, U.S. Navy; © Bill Pugliano, Getty Images; J.M. Eddins Jr., U.S. Air Force; Kippelboy (licensed under CC BY-SA 3.0)

14-15 © Andrey Popov, Shutterstock; © IBM

16-19 © Shutterstock

20-21 © Foto Away/Shutterstock; © SSPL/Getty Images; © Testing/Shutterstock; © Pirita/Shutterstock; © Piaggio Group

22-23 © Getty Images; © Arx Pax, LLC; © Universal Pictures; © Max Belchenko, Shutterstock

24-25 © Nnattalli/Shutterstock; © Lerner Vadim, Shutterstock; DEKA Research and Development Corp.

26-27 © Fitbit, Inc.; © Wearable Experiments

28-29 © Shutterstock

30-31 Public Domain; © SmartPlate; © UCLA; © Seregam/Shutterstock

32-33 © Ruki Media/Shutterstock; © Sleep Number Corporation; © Mechanix Illustrated; © Owlet Baby Care

34-35 © IKEA; © Natural Machines

36-37 © Andrey Popov, Shutterstock; © June Life Inc.; © LG Electronics; © SSPL/Getty Images

38-39 © Cholpan/Shutterstock; © Anki; © PullString, Inc.

40-41 © Chris Willson, Alamy Images; Public Domain (Evan Amos); © Wonder Workshop, Inc; © Sony Corporation

42-43 © RA 2 Studio/Shutterstock; © Bank of Canada

44-45 © Christopher Polk, Getty Images; © Looking Glass Factory, Inc.; © Light Field Lab; © CBS; © Nico El Nino/Shutterstock

www.ingramcontent.com/pod-product-compliance
Ingram Content Group UK Ltd.
Pitfield, Milton Keynes, MK11 3LW, UK
UKHW061957290726
14090UKWH00021B/1256

9 780716 625421